WOMEN WHO DARE

Amelia Earhart

BY SUSAN REYBURN

Pomegranate
SAN FRANCISCO

LIBRARY OF CONGRESS
WASHINGTON, DC

Published by Pomegranate Communications, Inc.
Box 808022, Petaluma CA 94975
800 227 1428; www.pomegranate.com

Pomegranate Europe Ltd.
Unit 1, Heathcote Business Centre, Hurlbutt Road
Warwick, Warwickshire CV34 6TD, UK
[+44] 0 1926 430111; sales@pomeurope.co.uk

Amy Pastan, Series Editor

In association with the Library of Congress, Pomegranate publishes other books in the Women Who Dare® series, as well as calendars, books of postcards, posters, and Knowledge Cards® featuring daring women. Please contact the publisher for more information.

Library of Congress Cataloging-in-Publication Data

Reyburn, Susan.
    Amelia Earhart / by Susan Reyburn.
      p. cm. — (Women who dare)
    Includes bibliographical references.
    ISBN 0-7649-3545-3
    1. Earhart, Amelia, 1897–1937. 2. Women air pilots—United States—Biography. 3. Air pilots—United States—Biography. I. Title. II. Women who dare (Petaluma, Calif.)

TL540.E3R49 2006
629.13092—dc22

2005054951

Pomegranate Catalog No. A111
Designed by Harrah Lord, Yellow House Studio, Rockport, ME
Printed in Korea

15 14 13 12 11 10 09 08 07 06   10 9 8 7 6 5 4 3 2 1

FRONT COVER: Earhart in the cockpit of a training plane, 1926.
The Schlesinger Library, Radcliffe Institute, Harvard University
BACK COVER: *Amelia Earhart*. Oil painting by Howard Chandler Christy, 1933.
Special Collections and Archives, Lafayette College

PREFACE

FOR TWO HUNDRED YEARS, the Library of Congress, the oldest national cultural institution in the United States, has been gathering materials necessary to tell the stories of women in America. The last third of the twentieth century witnessed a great surge of popular and scholarly interest in women's studies and women's history that has led to an outpouring of works in many formats. Drawing on women's history resources in the collections of the Library of Congress, the Women Who Dare book series is designed to provide readers with an entertaining introduction to the life of a notable American woman or a significant topic in women's history.

From its beginnings in 1800 as a legislative library, the Library of Congress has grown into a national library that houses both a universal collection of knowledge and the mint record of American creativity. Congress' decision to purchase Thomas Jefferson's personal library to replace the books and maps burned during the British occupation in 1814 set the Congressional Library on the path of collecting with the breadth of Jefferson's interests. Not just American imprints were to be acquired, but foreign-language materials as well, and Jefferson's library already included works by American and European women.

The Library of Congress has some 121 million items, largely housed in closed stacks in three buildings on Capitol Hill that contain twenty public reading rooms. The incredible, wide-ranging collections include books, maps, prints, newspapers, broadsides, diaries, letters, posters, musical scores, photographs, audio and video recordings, and documents available only in digital formats. The Library serves first-time users and the most experienced researchers alike.

I hope that you, the reader, will seek and find in the pages of this book information that will further your understanding of women's history. In addition, I hope you will continue to explore the topic of this book in a library near you, in person at the Library of Congress, or by visiting the Library on the World Wide Web at http://www.loc.gov. Happy reading!

—JAMES H. BILLINGTON, The Librarian of Congress

■ *Amelia Earhart, c. 1922.* LC-USZ62-45002

IN GALLAGHER'S PASTURE

Women must try to do things as men have tried. When they fail, their failure must be but a challenge to others.

—Amelia Earhart

T he day Amelia Earhart pointed her single-engined Lockheed Vega plane down the runway at Harbour Grace, Newfoundland, bound for Europe, the current issue of *Liberty* magazine featured an article by the renowned British aviator Lady Mary Heath, titled "Why I Believe Women Pilots Can't Fly the Atlantic." It was also the fifth anniversary to the day of Charles Lindbergh's 1927 solo flight across the same ocean, and no one else had completed the perilous trip alone since then. Lady Heath was convinced that any female attempt would be suicidal. Earhart thought her chances of landing safely on the other side might be one in ten. She also thought it would be fun.

And it was, except perhaps for flying blind in the fog, the storms that violently shook her plane, the failed altimeter, the leaking fuel gauge, the exhaust manifold that burned out. At one point the plane iced up and went into a tailspin, and when she regained control, Earhart had a disturbingly close view of ocean whitecaps below. She still had sufficient fuel to reach Paris, but with her plane in such a state, she headed for Ireland, then followed the railroad tracks to Londonderry. On the afternoon of

■ *Amelia Earhart's childhood home in Atchison, Kansas. She was born here on July 24, 1897.* THE SCHLESINGER LIBRARY, RADCLIFFE INSTITUTE, HARVARD UNIVERSITY

May 21, 1932, Dan McCallion, a farmhand, was startled to see a little red airplane circle and land in a gently sloping meadow, alarming his cattle. Emerging from the Vega after fifteen hours in the air, Earhart shouted out to him, "Where am I?"

"In Gallagher's pasture," McCallion answered, astonished at hearing a woman's voice. A moment later he asked, "Have you come far?"

"From America," she replied.

But she had come much farther than that.

■ *Sisters Muriel and Amelia Earhart, c. 1903, in Kansas City, Kansas.*

PERHAPS EARHART'S first thrill of high-speed, wind-in-her-hair excitement was aboard a rickety backyard roller coaster whose construction she oversaw, unknown to her parents, when she was seven years old. She and her sister, Muriel, were self-described tomboys who took to sports, horseback riding, and climbing trees, but young Amelia was also an avid reader. "I am sure I was a horrid little girl," she wrote in her 1932 book *The Fun of It.* "Perhaps the fact that I was exceedingly fond of reading made me endurable." In her early years, she was raised in Atchison, Kansas, mostly

■ *Front and center, Amelia is flanked by her sister, Muriel; uncle, Carl Otis; grandmother, Amelia Otis; aunt, Mrs. Carl Otis; mother, Amy Otis Earhart; and father, Edward Earhart, c. 1908–1910. Her parents divorced in 1924, and her father died six years later.*

■ *Earhart enrolled at the Orgontz School in 1916. The next year, following school tradition, she posed in commencement regalia on Halloween. She left Orgontz in February 1918 to take Red Cross training and did not actually graduate.*

THE SCHLESINGER LIBRARY, RADCLIFFE INSTITUTE, HARVARD UNIVERSITY

by her grandparents. Later, the Earhart family moved frequently throughout the Midwest as her alcoholic father slid from job to job and his career as a railroad lawyer deteriorated. In addition to the emotional and financial strain on the family, it meant, for Amelia, attending six high schools before graduating from Chicago's Hyde Park High School in 1915.

After high school, Amelia enrolled at the upscale Orgontz finishing school near Philadelphia. In letters to her mother she wrote of taking

■ *Earhart in 1918, the last year of World War I, while working with the Canadian Red Cross as a nurse's aide at the Spadina Military Convalescent Hospital.*

German, French, modern drama, literature, art, and Bible study. The school headmistress would recall her as a questioning student who "sought out the challenging authors: Shaw, Dreiser, Dostoevsky" and that when outside for military drill, "no airplane drone on the farthest horizon failed to claim her attention." Earhart reported in the fall of 1917 that "I am Vice President of the class. . . .Then I am secretary by popular vote to a Red Cross chapter we are organizing. . . . Then I am secretary and treasurer of Christian Endeavor—no sinecure. It has been rather an institution of torture heretofore, and not well liked but we are trying to . . . make it stand for something. . . . I am elected too to write the senior song, but you know the more one does, the more one can do." She backed the administration when it banned secret societies, chastising her uncooperative classmates for violating a "moral code," and led an effort to acquire less expensive class rings. Somehow she found time for field hockey, swimming, and basketball, proudly writing home on one occasion "I played Hockey again to-day and a made a goal thru my legs which convulsed on-lookers." Although unsure what career path she would take, for inspiration and future reference she kept a scrapbook titled "Activities of Women," pasting in newspaper and magazine clippings about accomplished women in nontraditional professions.

Earhart left Orgontz in February 1918, following a visit with her sister at St. Margaret's College in Toronto. There she had seen something that "changed the course of existence for me." She wrote of watching four Canadian World War I veterans "on crutches, doing their heart-breakingly best to walk together down King Street . . . and it came home to me then that war wasn't knitting sweaters and selling Liberty bonds. . . . The Canadian Red Cross took me in training and I qualified as a nurse's aid." She was employed in the Spadina Military Convalescent Hospital dispensary—in part because she had studied chemistry, but she also figured the fact that "I could be trusted not to drink up the medical supply of whisky counted more than the chemistry." The experience led her to become a pre-medical student at Columbia University in 1919, as well as an ardent pacifist.

After a year she left Columbia and followed her parents, who urged

■ *Flying instructor Anita "Neta" Snook, left, with Earhart at the Beverly Hills Speedway, July 16, 1921. Behind them is Earhart's first plane, a $2,000 Kinner Airster; she called it a Kinner Canary for its bright yellow color. When she sold the plane three years later, the young purchaser and his passenger were killed in a crash the first time he flew it.*

her to resettle with them in Los Angeles. She became a fixture at the local air meets that were filling Southern California's skies with inexpensive surplus military planes from World War I. Engine-powered flight was still new—even younger than twenty-three-year-old Earhart—and the death toll among pilots was alarmingly high. In December 1920 pilot Frank Hawks took her on her first plane ride; exhilarated, she claimed she would just die if she could not learn to fly. She signed up for lessons she could

■ *Earhart's wheels were nearly as swift as her wings. She called her 1922 Kissel Gold-bug car the Yellow Peril, and in 1924 she and her mother drove it from Los Angeles to Boston by way of Seattle and nearly every national park in between. When they reached Boston, Earhart wrote, the car "had so many tourist stickers on the windshield there was little space left to see through it."*

ill afford and got her first job, working as a clerk in a telephone office. Earhart recounted that among her responsibilities, she "did things to the mail; filed letters and then tried to find them."

Anita "Neta" Snook was only twenty-four years old when she taught Earhart how to fly at Kinner Field. After six hours of in-flight instruction, Earhart soloed, and as Snook later described the scene, "Her first solo flight gave us quite a scare. . . .When she landed she headed for the far

■ *Seen here with immigrant children in front of Denison House, in Boston, Earhart was a popular social worker, and her car often drew a crowd. "She frequently let as many as ten children climb in and stand on the running boards while she drove slowly around the block," her sister recalled. "For many of them it was their first ride in an automobile." The car's loud yellow color, Earhart noted, "had been modest enough in California, but was a little outspoken in Boston."*

■ *After a fogbound flight of nearly twenty-one hours from Trepassey, Newfoundland, to Burry Port, Wales, the trimotor Fokker* Friendship *makes a pontoon landing at nearby Southampton, England (its original destination), June 19, 1928.* GETTY IMAGES

end of the field. Two telegraph poles were right in front of her. We held our breath—but she flew between the poles and landed safely!" Another witness told her she had landed "rottenly," and Earhart herself admitted that her first effort ended with "an exceptionally poor landing." But, as early aviators frequently reminded themselves, "If you can walk away, it was a good landing." She bought her first plane six months later with family financing. "It took all her savings—and mine," said her sister. Their mother chipped in as well, and her uncle, A. M. Earhart, reluctantly

EARHART'S GUIDE
TO THE AVIATRIX ENSEMBLE

Early in her flying career, Earhart donned the requisite helmet, goggles, boots, and leather jacket, and she gardened and slept in her new jacket to wrinkle and "age" it. For long-distance night flights, she usually wore fleece- or fur-lined leather coveralls. Like many other female pilots of her time, Earhart preferred to wear men's briefs under her flying clothes rather than women's underwear, which made relieving oneself in a cramped cockpit an even greater acrobatic challenge. As daring as she was, Earhart could not bring herself to purchase men's jockey shorts in department stores, so her friend Eugene Vidal (father of the author Gore Vidal) bought them for her.

Earhart later discarded the once-practical "aviation costumes," preferring to wear street clothes when she flew (many newer planes had enclosed cockpits). But in April 1933, after attending a formal dinner with Eleanor Roosevelt in Washington, DC, she took the new First Lady flying while still in her long evening gown and high-heeled shoes. An Associated Press newswoman aboard the plane reported that Earhart took the controls "without even removing her white evening gloves."

■ *Earhart in her aviation apparel, 1928.* GETTY IMAGES

contributed four hundred dollars toward what he thought was a "silly" purchase and "the height of folly."

For the next several years, Earhart racked up flight time and experience flying in air rodeos, stunting, and holding a string of jobs. She was a photographer, truck driver, and co-owner of a sand and gravel company before moving back to the East Coast and resuming her studies at Columbia. (In 1932, she noted, "I've had 28 different jobs in my life and I hope I'll have 228 more. . . . By adventuring about, you become accustomed to the unexpected. The unexpected then becomes what it really is—the inevitable.") Despite having no experience in social work, she was recommended for, and accepted, a position at Denison House, a settlement house in Boston for immigrants. On one occasion she flew over the city dropping handbills to advertise a fund-raiser for Denison. "Later I learned the police were on my trail for 'wantonly littering the streets of Boston,'" she told her sister. "They never caught me, though."

Meanwhile, Amy Guest, a wealthy American living in Britain, hoped to be the first woman to fly across the Atlantic Ocean—that is, until her family, horrified at the idea, refused to allow it. She agreed to sponsor the flight if a "suitable" American woman took her place as passenger. Through a series of connections between the indefatigable publisher George Palmer Putnam (known as GP), an adventurer with an acute sense for public relations, and the Boston Aviation Association, the flying social worker was given the chance to risk her life for "a grand adventure" and the opportunity to write about it afterward. Joining top pilot Wilmer Stultz and mechanic Lou "Slim" Gordon aboard a trimotor Fokker seaplane dubbed the *Friendship,* Earhart departed from Newfoundland on

■ *(Left to right) Amy Guest, flight sponsor; Lou "Slim" Gordon, mechanic; Amelia Earhart, designated flight commander; Wilmer Stultz, pilot; and Lucia Marion Welch, mayor of Southampton, celebrate after the* Friendship's *historic transatlantic flight. In London, Earhart stayed with Mrs. Guest, did some emergency shopping ("All the baggage I brought was my toothbrush and what I'm wearing" explained Earhart when still in her flight suit), and was fêted all over the city. A little more than a year after this photo was taken, Stultz died in a plane crash. Earhart attended his funeral in New York.* CORBIS

■ *A week after the* Friendship *flight and the subsequent blur of engagements (including visits to Wimbledon, Ascot, and Parliament), Earhart was back in her natural habitat. She slipped away from her hostess and her manager to try out the Avro Avian Moth aircraft at London's Croyden Field, piloting the Moth over the Thames and the English Channel. Upon landing, she bought the plane and brought it aboard the SS* Roosevelt *when she returned to the United States.* GETTY IMAGES

June 17, 1928. When the *Friendship* safely touched down in Burry Port, Wales, near Southampton, the next day, Earhart, thrilled to make the flight but disappointed that she had not done any of the piloting, was at the center of international attention and all the group photos. "Wanting to fly was the reason I took my first job," she later wrote. "Wanting others to fly

■ *Amelia Earhart with her mother, Amy Otis Earhart, at a reception in Boston for the Friendship fliers, July 9, 1928. "We have flown a lot together, my child and I," said Mrs. Earhart in 1935. "Sometime soon I'm going to get her to fly across the sea with me. Which sea? Oh, it doesn't matter much."* LC-USZ62-66659

was one reason why I undertook to share this Atlantic flight."

The fact that a woman dared to fly the treacherous Atlantic, long a graveyard to sailors and now to aviators, was regarded as astonishing and praiseworthy. As the *New York Times* correspondent in London reported, "The deaths of [aviators] Princess Lowenstein-Wertheim and Miss Elsie

Mackaye are still so recent in the British popular mind that until Miss Earhart's arrival opinion had hardened in opposition to woman passengers in transatlantic flights." Accepting the very real possibility that she might not survive the attempt either, Earhart had made out a will and left "popping off" letters for her family in case she did not return. (To her mother she wrote: "Even though I have lost, the adventure was worthwhile. . . . My life has really been very happy, and I didn't mind contemplating its end in the midst of it." To her father: "Dearest Dad: Hooray for

■ *Earhart spent the summer of 1931 promoting autogiros for the Beech-Nut Company. Seen here at a stop in Denver, she met with* Denver Post *publisher Frederick Bonfils and mingled with the ever-present news media.*

the last grand adventure! I wish I had won, but it was worthwhile, anyway. You know that. I have no faith we'll meet anywhere again, but I wish we might.")

At every opportunity, Earhart heralded her colleagues' performance and downplayed her own participation: "I was a passenger on the journey—just a passenger. Everything that was done to bring us across was done by Wilmer Stultz and Slim Gordon. Any praise I can give them they ought to have. You can't pile it on too thick." Had she done nothing else with the rest of her life, Earhart had secured a place in aviation history, but she wanted to earn the accolades given her after the flight. "The next time I fly anywhere, I shall do it alone!" she declared, crawling out from under the mountainous praise that was heaped on her.

Earhart flew whenever she could, competed in races, participated in Zonta—a service organization for businesswomen—and for the next eight years, under Putnam's management, delivered compelling sold-out presentations on the national lecture circuit. She also maintained a steady presence on the newsstand, writing aviation articles for *Cosmopolitan* and major newspapers. She spent 1931 experimenting with Harold Pitcairn's new line of autogiros, which could hover, land in compact spaces, and, some suggested, replace the family car. Earhart soloed in one after just a few minutes of in-flight instruction. "Thinking over the moment when the autogiro rose into the air," she later wrote, "I am at a loss now to say whether I flew it or it flew me." She set an autogiro altitude record (18,415 feet) in April, and that summer embarked on promotional cross-country flights for the Beech-Nut Company. Unfortunately, the autogiros remained difficult to handle, and Earhart had several ugly landings. In Abilene, Texas, she was caught up in a windstorm on takeoff, plummeting into several parked cars, but avoiding spectators. The Department of Commerce issued her a written reprimand, but, as Earhart wrote to her mother, "The reprimand wasn't one really. . . . I am not a careless pilot and the letter doesn't say so."

By 1932, Earhart was ready to conquer the Atlantic alone, no matter what Lady Heath had to say about it.

THE FIRST WOMEN'S
NATIONAL AIR DERBY

■ *The elite of the field pose on the opening day of the first Women's National Air Derby, August 18, 1929, in Santa Monica, California. (Left to right) Louise Thaden, Bobbie Trout, Patty Willis, Marvel Crosson, Blanche Noyes, Vera Dawn Walker, Amelia Earhart, Marjorie Crawford, Ruth Elder, and Florence Lowe Barnes. Thaden won the nine-day, 2,350-mile race to Cleveland, Earhart finished third, and Crosson died in the Arizona desert after bailing out of her malfunctioning plane. In Cleveland, the competitors discussed Earhart and Ruth Nichols' plan to create a female pilots' organization. Dubbed "The Ninety-Nines" for its number of members, the group formed in November 1929 and Earhart was elected its first president in 1932.* CORBIS

■ *Amelia Earhart, aka "First Lady of the Air." Known as AE to friends and family, Earhart usually carried a fanciful appellation in the press, such as "Girl Flier," "Girl Air Bird," "Sky Tourist," "Lady Lindy" (a reference to Charles "Lucky Lindy" Lindbergh), and "Queen of the Air," among others. By the mid-1930s her name in headlines was usually "Miss Earhart," which she preferred, or "Mrs. Putnam."*

LIBRARY OF CONGRESS, GENERAL COLLECTIONS

"I WANT TO DO
WHAT I WANT TO DO"

Tradition has been a terrible handicap for women," Earhart remarked in 1933. "Sometimes I think tradition is the hardest obstacle we have to fight. I actually know men and women who not only are surprised that I can fly, but are surprised that women can do anything interesting." Not one to buck tradition merely for its own sake, Earhart simply bypassed conventions that dictated what women should study or wear and how they ought to conduct their lives when such practices contradicted her own choices. As the August 1935 edition of the *Farmer's Wife* observed—ironically, given the publication's name—"She is Amelia Earhart, Incorporated, and no one else."

The press described her as "slender," with "tousled hair," and her hands were the subject of frequent comment (the *New York World Telegram and Sun* called them "delicate looking and exquisitely manicured," while the *New York Times* said she had "fingers like an artist's"; George Putnam, whom she would marry, said the "loveliness of her hands was almost unbelievable"). Hating the way her ankles looked, she was more than happy to keep them hidden under a long pair of pants whenever possible. Mrs. Earhart once referred to her oldest daughter—then thirty-seven years old—as "a good child, unspoiled," and she supported Amelia's aviation career. (Mr. Earhart had been less enthusiastic.) Within Amelia's calm, quiet interior flourished a whimsical nature, exhibited in the vocabulary

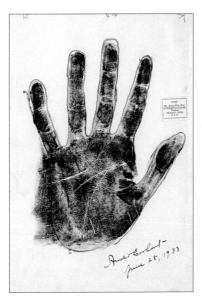

■ *Palm reader Nellie Simmons, who analyzed the palm prints of well-known figures, took this print from Earhart on June 28, 1933; the pilot signed it. Simmons reported that "The length of the palm indicates the love of physical activity" and that "the length of the fingers, indicative of carefulness in detail . . . acts as a preventive to her taking unnecessary risks or doing foolhardy stunts."*

LIBRARY OF CONGRESS, MANUSCRIPT DIVISION

and spelling she used in private correspondence. An excellent student, she occasionally responded with a bit of French poetry when stymied on college physics exams. (She once waved off her academic success by saying that it was "No credit to me. My I.Q. is low enough to ensure natural cheerfulness.")

In her early twenties, Earhart subtracted a year from her age and kept it off, and she produced a highly embellished résumé when she applied for a job through the Women's Educational and Industrial Union; what she lacked in experience and qualifications she made up for

■ *A veteran lecturer, Earhart spoke at a luncheon in her honor at the Criterion in London two days after her solo Atlantic flight, to the delight of reporters and various dignitaries, including Aimée de Fleuriau, the French ambassador (left), and Andrew Mellon, the American ambassador (second from right). Having once again arrived in Britain in a plane packed with fuel tanks but no luggage, Earhart borrowed clothes from Ailsa Mellon Bruce, Ambassador Mellon's daughter and US embassy hostess, until she could pick up some new outfits.* GETTY IMAGES

with confidence. Some found her quiet; others regarded her manner as aloof, but she was warm and generous to friends and the media. She doted on her youngest relatives and provided significant financial support to her extended family. As the only family member with a knack for managing money, Earhart repeatedly made it clear that she disapproved of what appeared to her as Muriel's chaotic household and of her mother's recklessly open hand. ("Please don't give it all away if the giving means fostering dependence and lack of responsibility," she chided her mother in a 1933 letter.)

Earhart was an avid gardener, but despised housework. She was partial to buttermilk and homegrown vegetables, and once remarked that "I think I myself can eat anything but oatmeal." (Her in-flight fare, even on long-distance flights, was spare: tomato juice, hot cocoa, hard-boiled eggs, malted milk tablets.) Chronically intrigued by political and social possibilities that might advance civilization, she endorsed President Roosevelt in the 1936 campaign. She was also open to unconventional ideas, sharing an interest in psychic phenomena with her friend Jackie Cochrane, another aviation legend. A lifelong student, Earhart developed an agnostic outlook as a young adult and later, when asked by another pilot if she prayed during serious flight trouble, said that she did not, believing it "unsportsmanlike" to call upon a deity only when in a crisis. Despite her voluminous writings and easy manner with all types of people—heads of state, film stars, reporters, immigrants, children, or that excitable, curious mass that was the public—she always remained private and seldom shared confidences with even those closest to her.

Amelia Mary Earhart required—and got—full partnership in her marriage (complete with an escape clause, which she never exercised) to George Palmer Putnam (GP), who proposed at least a half-dozen times before she accepted in the fall of 1930. The day of their wedding, Earhart handed her fiancé a four-page prenuptial agreement. Knowing her as he did, GP was not the least bit fazed that she would keep her independence, her career, her options, and her name: it was part of her appeal.

Dear Gyp,

There are some things which should be writ before we are married—things we have talked over before—most of them.

You must know again my reluctance to marry, my feeling that I shatter thereby chances in work which mean most to me. I feel the move just now as foolish as anything I could do. I know there may be compensations but have no heart to look ahead.

On our life together I want you to understand I shall not hold you to any medieval code of faithfulness to me nor shall I consider myself bound to you similarly. If we can be honest I think the difficulties which arise may best be avoided should you or I become interested deeply (or in passing) in anyone else.

Please let us not interfere with the other's work or play, nor let the world see our private joys or disagreements. In this connection I may have to keep some place where I can go to be myself now and then, for I cannot guarantee to endure at all times the confinement of even an attractive cage.

I must exact a cruel promise and that is you will let me go in a year if we find no happiness together.

I will try to do my best in every way and give you that part of me you know and seem to want.

—A.E.

After her 1932 solo Atlantic flight, Earhart said, "My husband is a good sport. He does not interfere with my flying and I don't interfere with his [business] affairs." "After all," as GP once observed, "I'm related to aviation only by marriage." This wasn't entirely the case—their work became intertwined. He relentlessly promoted her career, causing resentment among some pilots who, not being married to their own one-man publicity machine, did not receive the attention they warranted or wanted. And Earhart took advantage of the buzz he created as a way to maintain her very expensive avocation and to garner public and government support for aviation. But her comment did reflect a finely honed sense of equality—she and GP evenly split the costs of running their household—that extended well beyond her personal life. In 1930, she led a group of top women fliers in boycotting the second National Women's Air Derby when the sponsors established restrictions in the women's competition (including limits on the size and speed of their aircraft) that were not applied to the men's event.

As a visiting faculty member and women's career adviser at Purdue University, Earhart encouraged young women to pursue careers of their own choosing and not to rush into marriage—advice that rattled male students and at least one instructor. GP quoted a professor as saying that if Earhart kept at it, "the coeds won't be willing to get married and lead the quiet life for which Nature intended them." Such strictures rankled her for the sake of both sexes, whether they kept boys out of cooking classes or girls out of engineering classes. When Earhart spoke to the Daughters of the American Revolution in Washington, DC, in 1933 (after warning them that they should not invite her), the audience gasped when she faulted them for vigorously issuing resolutions supporting a large national

■ *Earhart peruses a stack of congratulatory telegrams at the small cottage of farmhand Dan McCallion (far left), the only witness to her arrival in Gallagher's pasture, near Londonderry, Ireland, where she ended her 1932 solo transatlantic flight. She spent her first night in Ireland at the Gallaghers' farmhouse; on the following day, hundreds gathered to see her land the Vega in the field once more, for the movie cameras. In March 1933, the Ulster-Irish Society in New York presented Earhart with a roll of fine linen woven from flax grown in Gallagher's pasture.*

LIBRARY OF CONGRESS, GENERAL COLLECTIONS

defense without offering to serve in the military themselves. "Equality with men is essential in all lines," she said, before dropping her own bombshell. "Women should be drafted in war as well as men." In 1935 she wrote: "How often we have heard a woman say, 'I gave my son, but I would gladly have gone in his place—if they had only let me.' Would she, really? If she is telling the truth, then I say, in the next war, let her."

First Lady Eleanor Roosevelt credited Earhart with opening many doors for women, whether or not welcome mats were in place. In 1934, Earhart noted that there were forty men for every woman in the aviation industry. "But more will enter as a greater number knock at the door," she said, adding, "It may be well to bring an axe along, as you might have to chop down the door." Ultimately, in Earhart's view, all women deserved the opportunities available to men; only then could female suitability for various professions be determined. "What I say is that conclusions should not be drawn until women are given equal chances with men in training, experience, and equipment and until the same number of them are doing the things that men are doing. This has never been done in flying," she pointed out. "I am not even sure it has been done in pie making."

Beyond advocating roles for women in aviation, Earhart tirelessly pushed the industry itself: aviation should be more than thrill rides and stunting, more than military hardware. It should become an integral component of mail delivery, cargo transport, and passenger service. On several occasions she testified before Congress on the importance of supporting the fledgling airline business, declaring in 1934, "Aviation is a young and struggling industry. Care must be taken not to kill it before it can even

■ *New York City gives Earhart a rousing reception and a ticker tape parade following her solo Atlantic flight, June 20, 1932.*

develop." Two years later she told a Senate congressional committee, "I am proud of the industry, and all that it has done in its few years, but the balloon is deflated when I reflect that the airplane transport business compares in size with the button industry."

The public's reluctance to embrace commercial air travel in the late 1920s and early 1930s was no doubt traceable to highly publicized airline crashes that left no survivors. Earhart herself flew almost daily

■ *President and Mrs. Hoover present Earhart with the National Geographic Society's Special Medal for her "courage and achievement" on June 21, 1932, the first time the honor went to a woman. Dr. Gilbert Grosvenor, NGS president, is at left; GP is behind the president. A formal presentation in Constitution Hall was made that evening, and the next day the US Congress voted to award her the Distinguished Flying Cross.*

LC-USZ62-20705

aboard the New York, Philadelphia, and Washington Airway line in 1930 as a company vice president. She tried to allay fears by telling listeners that automobile travel at more than fifty miles per hour was more dangerous than flying, and that her mother, a frequent flier, was so comfort-

■ *A Consolidated Fleetster of the New York, Philadelphia and Washington Airway Corporation (aka Ludington Lines) circles the US Capitol, giving passengers a spectacular view. In 1930 Earhart accepted a position as company vice president, overseeing publicity, managing its complaint department, and encouraging women and families to fly.*
LC-USZ62-74129

able in the air that she actually spent the time reading (as opposed, presumably, to gripping her seat in terror). After losing a friend, the aviation pioneer Wiley Post, to a crash in 1935, Earhart defended dangerous experimental flights as necessary for progress. "Of course there are some

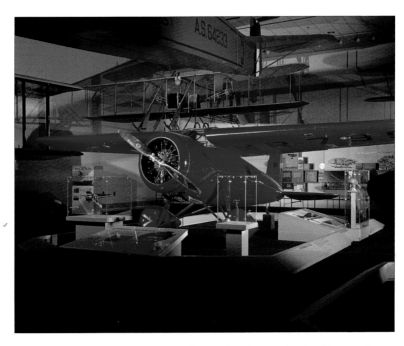

■ *Earhart called this Lockheed 5B Vega her "Little Red Bus"; she piloted it across the Atlantic Ocean and nonstop across the continental United States in 1932. It is a featured attraction at the Smithsonian's National Air and Space Museum, in Washington, DC.*

■ *GP and AE spent Christmas 1934 aboard the* Lurline *en route to Honolulu, where Earhart would begin a 2,400-mile overnight flight to Oakland, California. Her new Lockheed Vega, seen here being hoisted from the ship, "is perched on the aft tennis deck and excites considerable interest," Earhart wrote her mother. "A couple of elderly ladies are sure it's going to be flown off the ship and they are planning to be on hand for the event."* LC-USZ62-110858

accidents," she said at the time. "But look at the automobile accidents. Look at the fatal accidents from dozens of causes. Living itself is full of hazards. To live life fully requires courage to take some risks. At least that's the way I see it."

In January 1935, Earhart became the first person to fly solo from Hawaii to California. The flight was the easy part; more difficult was dealing with those who disapproved of the endeavor. Only a month earlier, Charles Ulm and his crew had died in the Pacific while flying from California to Hawaii. An editorial in Honolulu's *Star-Bulletin*, reprinted nationwide, stated that "If Amelia intends to fly solo from Hawaii to the mainland, responsible authorities should stop her from doing it. . . . Even if she is successful, nothing beyond what is known would be proved. If she fails, the ghastly Ulm search would be repeated." The day after arriving safely in Oakland, Earhart responded to her critics: "The flight from Honolulu was attempted with no thought of proving anything aeronautical," she wrote. "I can only hope one more passage across that portion of the Pacific succeeds in marking a little more plainly the pathway over which the inevitable air service of the future will fly. To me, also, it seemed good training for other hoped-for long-distance flights. . . ." She continued to win over her critics. As GP noted in his account of her takeoff from Honolulu in the presence of military airmen, "In the tense seconds while the ship wallowed along, gaining speed ever so slowly, I daresay the coolest person within a mile of it was the hundred-twenty-pound pilot, concentrating all she had, to fight those three tons of weight safely off the ground. Of course she got off—with two thousand yards of

■ *A crowd swarms to greet Earhart upon her landing in Oakland on January 12, 1935, and becoming the first person ever to fly solo across the Pacific Ocean from Hawaii to California. She was startled by the welcome from more than ten thousand well-wishers, noting that "thousands of people were waiting to see a bedraggled pilot climb out of an airplane." GP sent his wife a congratulatory message from Hawaii: "Swell job. Hope it doesn't become a habit." Awaiting his return by ship, Earhart wrote in her newspaper story about the flight that her husband "is on the high seas bound for San Francisco, vastly irritated at my having taken a short cut, leaving him to travel the long way."*

THE SCHLESINGER LIBRARY, RADCLIFFE INSTITUTE, HARVARD UNIVERSITY

■ *Seen here observing a botany class, Earhart arrived as a visiting faculty member at Purdue University in the fall of 1935.*

field to spare—to the amazement of a major who feels that women really shouldn't do such unfeminine things and darned near kissed me with delight when she did."

Earhart won over young people as well, such as seventeen-year-old Mary Walker of Newark, the first female member of the Bamberger Aero Club in 1935. Walker planned a career in aviation journalism, saying her interest "could either be blamed on or attributed to Amelia Earhart, who has inspired so many others by her wonderful feats." The Earhart Effect

could last a lifetime. Helen Jane Williams of Minneapolis, who was sixteen when she attended an Earhart lecture, recalled nearly seventy years later that it was one of the most thrilling events of her youth, because "Here was a woman doing things nobody else I knew was doing. Her life was so exciting."

■ *Orville Wright, the first person to fly a motorized aircraft, and Earhart at Philadelphia's Benjamin Franklin Institute, December 17, 1933, on the thirtieth anniversary of the Wright brothers' inaugural flight. Earhart's Vega is displayed above the two aviation pioneers (it was later moved to the National Air and Space Museum). In August 1932, Earhart wrote to Wright from the Ambassador Hotel in Los Angeles to tell him that she had "had the fun of cracking a bottle of gasoline on the nose of a new automobile"—an Essex Terraplane he had ordered from the Hudson Motor Company—adding that "my fun was increased when I found that the one I christened was for you."*

■ *Earhart confers with a contractor on expanding and remodeling the small house she and GP bought in North Hollywood, where they planned to settle permanently.*

■ *"Clothes for Women Who Live Actively!"* was the tag line for Amelia Earhart Fashions. Earhart designed suits, dresses, slacks, blouses (made with parachute silk), hats, and jackets for her clothing line, carried in thirty major department stores nationwide, beginning with Macy's in New York City. She did some promotional modeling, and later developed her own luggage line.

■ *GP and AE near their home in Rye, New York, c. 1936.*

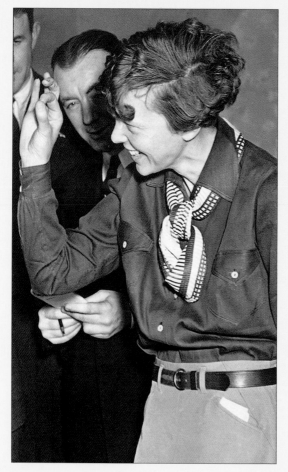

■ *While preparing for her round-the-world flight, Earhart responds to a reporter's question with a gesture suggesting Howland Island's tiny size. She knew that reaching the central Pacific island—less than two miles long and only a half-mile wide—would be the most dangerous and difficult part of her flight.*

LIBRARY OF CONGRESS

FINAL FLIGHT

I t is unfortunate that in the twenty-first century Amelia Earhart is better known to many for her disappearance than for the achievements that merited her public appearance in the first place. She was an extraordinary figure—routinely on the annual lists of most admired women, the recipient of numerous honors and bags of fan mail. She was not merely the best-known pilot among other women making landmark flights; in the 1930s, she was among the best-known and most photographed women in the world.

Throughout her adult life, she took on jobs to keep flying, and she flew because she loved it. She would often say, "Pilots love to fly because of the beauty of flight—whether they know it or not." In 1935, she described the experience of flying over the Gulf of Mexico: "There were a lot of thunderstorms just beginning to stick up their heads. I cut around the edges of these black thunder-heads that had purple lightning inside of them, and all I could think was, 'How pretty my ship must look against such a background,' and there was nobody there to see it." She reveled in the challenges and silences of long-distance flying. The *Washington Post* reported in July 1932 that "A few minutes before she took off [from Los Angeles], an anxious spectator inquired if she really intended to fly to New York alone. 'Yes, I do,' she said with a smile. 'I need that extra weight for gasoline rather than somebody to talk to.'"

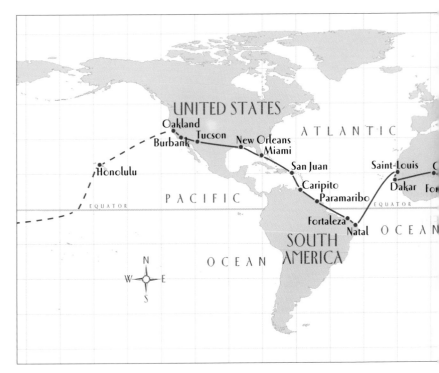

■ *THE ROUTE AROUND THE WORLD, JUNE 1–JULY 2, 1937. Earhart quietly began her second global attempt in Oakland on May 21, working her way east to Miami for the official beginning of the world flight. She and her navigator had flown 22,000 miles and had about 5,000 to go when they disappeared. The pair was expected in Oakland, California, on the Fourth of July.*

MAP BY TAMMY WONG, GEOGRAPHY AND MAP DIVISION, LIBRARY OF CONGRESS, AND MARIAH LANDER

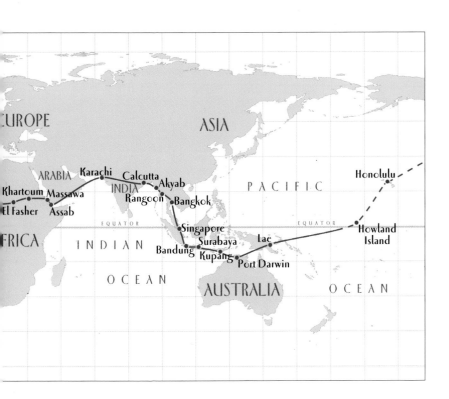

■ *A mechanic shows Earhart his work on one of her new Lockheed Electra's engines. She had excellent technical knowledge of all her planes, but was also wise enough to get out of her crew's way after explaining exactly what it was she wanted done.*

Early in 1937, Earhart told reporters that "I think I have just one more long flight in my system." It would be the culmination of her professional life's work: circumnavigating the globe at its greatest width—around the equator—which had never been done before. She also recognized that such a venture might be her last flight ever. "Decide . . . whether or not the goal is worth the risks involved," she advised others. "If it is, stop worrying." She took her own advice. With GP and a team

■ *The Lockheed Electra's cockpit measured only four feet six inches wide, four feet six inches deep, and four feet eight inches high—certainly roomier than those in Earhart's earlier planes—but was equipped with the latest aviation technology. At the time, only Earhart and Howard Hughes privately owned Lockheed Electra 10E aircraft.*
LC-USZ62-119492

of technical experts, Earhart expended immense energy preparing for the flight, and in July 1936 she took possession of a new Lockheed Electra 10E, a gift from a Purdue University research foundation. Her first round-the-world attempt in March 1937 ended with a crash in Hawaii on takeoff. ("I've seen and participated in many crashes," said Brigadier General Barton K. Yount, "but I never saw anybody come out of one so coolly as she has.") Disappointed but not deterred, Earhart and her husband raised more funds and tried again. As she wrote to Purdue's president, "Our second attempt is assured. We are solvent. Future is mortgaged, but what else are futures for?"

The second attempt officially began in Miami on June 1, 1937, in the repaired Electra, with expert navigator Fred Noonan on board. Safely out over the Atlantic just after six AM, Earhart soon tuned in to WQAM, in Miami, and heard "a breathlessly exciting" account of her very routine departure, as if it were live. "[J]ust then the radio station was sending out

■ *Earhart and her good friend Eugene Vidal, former director of the US Department of Commerce's Air Bureau, test the bright orange kites she planned to use as distress signals in a case of an accident on her round-the-world flight.*

LIBRARY OF CONGRESS, L'AÉROPHILE COLLECTION, SCIENCE, TECHNOLOGY AND BUSINESS DIVISION

■ *Earhart and three crew members pass serenely over the San Francisco Bay in her Lockheed Electra, heading into the vast, azure realm of the Pacific late in the day on March 17, 1937. This flight was the first leg of her attempt to circumnavigate the world via the equator. Two days later, an accident on takeoff in Hawaii postponed the global adventure until June.* PHOTO BY CLYDE SUNDERLAND

a description of my own take-off, which to me was quite too entertaining to miss," she wrote soon after. " . . . So, a hundred miles out from the field, the announcer held me in cruel suspense as to whether or not I actually was going to get off safely!" She and Noonan were airborne anywhere from five to fifteen hours a day as they made their way south to the eastern bulge of Brazil, over the South Atlantic, across Africa, and over Southeast Asia to Lae, New Guinea. From there they would fly 2,556 miles to tiny Howland Island, the only available place to refuel before reaching Hawaii. Earhart had regularly sent home articles on the flight's progress, and just before leaving New Guinea, she wrote that "Not more than a month ago I was on the other shore of the Pacific, looking westward. This evening I look eastward over the Pacific. In those fast moving days which have intervened, the whole width of the world has passed behind us—except this broad ocean. I shall be glad when we have the hazards of its navigation behind us."

Earhart and Noonan left Lae expecting an eighteen-hour flight to Howland, with the US Coast Guard ship *Itasca* nearby to provide radio contact. Noonan was unable to set his chronometers to his satisfaction, and after twenty hours in the air they had still not spotted the island. Nor could the Electra and *Itasca* establish effective two-way radio communication; despite all the preflight planning, there were crucial misunderstandings about broadcasting schedules, the Electra's radio equipment, and what frequencies Earhart was using.

They never landed on the island. The US Navy launched a massive, futile search, covering 250,000 square miles over sixteen days. Commander Warner Thompson, the *Itasca*'s captain, concluded that the Electra ran out of gas within a hundred miles of Howland Island and that Earhart and Noonan were lost at sea.

■ *AE and GP, after a private goodbye in the airport, have a last farewell before she departs Miami on June 1, 1937, officially beginning her second—and last—round-the-world attempt.* COURTESY PURDUE UNIVERSITY LIBRARIES ARCHIVES AND SPECIAL COLLECTIONS

■ *Earhart and navigator Fred Noonan, former head of Pan Am airline's navigation school, consult a map before the second round-the-world attempt. Noonan was considered one of the best celestial navigators in the world.*
CORBIS

■ *Fed and refueled in San Juan, Puerto Rico, Noonan and Earhart board the Electra, bound for Caripito, Venezuela.*
LC-USZ62-131169

WHETHER THE FLIGHT was foolhardy and pointless, as critics claimed, or justified in the pursuit of science, as others contended, mattered little to Earhart. As she explained in the summer of 1932, to those who found the purpose of her Atlantic flight incomprehensible, "Have you ever longed to go to the North Pole? . . . Or coast down a steep, snow-covered hill to an unknown valley? . . . Or, just before a thunderstorm, to turn ten somersaults on the lawn?" She could have added, "Or fly around the world in a way no one has done before?" Earhart believed her restless, ambitious spirit could endure the future only if she met this remaining challenge. A woman who kept her thoughts to herself, Earhart made no secret of the fact that however full her life might be, she was not looking forward to old age. She also suspected that she might never live to see it. Of all the possible ways to depart the earth that she had always marveled at while in flight, she hoped that whenever death came, she would be in her plane. Such a fate came to pass in the Pacific Ocean, and as the *New York Times* opined in July 1937, "Perhaps in the vividness of her last glimpse of sun and sky and the curling tops of the waves she knew that she had helped to make all women less afraid." ■

THE FIRST TO KNOW HER FATE

Albert Bresnik—Earhart's personal photographer, whom she fondly regarded as a younger brother—took this portrait in 1937; an enlarged version was on display in his Los Angeles studio at the time of her global flight. It drew the attention of a visiting German doctor, a member of the obscure National Church of Positive Christianity. As Bresnik would tell the author more than fifty years later, the doctor studied Earhart's image and announced that "The life force has gone out of that picture." Disturbed by the encounter, Bresnik called George Putnam, who had spoken with Earhart in New Guinea before she departed for Howland Island. GP assured Bresnik that everything was fine and not to worry. The next day, Bresnik heard the chilling news on his radio that Earhart was missing. "I knew right then," he recalled, "that she wasn't coming back."

PHOTO BY ALBERT BRESNIK

■ *The* Washington Post, *July 3, 1937. Reports of radio messages and signals from the Electra kept up hopes that Earhart and Noonan would be found alive. On January 5, 1939, a Los Angeles court declared Amelia Earhart legally dead.*

■ *On July 24, 1963—on what would have been Amelia Earhart's sixty-sixth birthday—the US Postal Service issued a commemorative airmail stamp in her honor.*

THE SCHLESINGER LIBRARY, RADCLIFFE INSTITUTE, HARVARD UNIVERSITY

■ *Looking relaxed and ready shortly before her second round-the-world attempt, Earhart had told reporters that after circumnavigating the globe, she would turn her attention to "My lovely home in North Hollywood—California sunshine—books— friends—leisurely travel—many things."*

ADDITIONAL READING AND SOURCES

Library Collections

Amelia Earhart Birthplace Museum, Atchison, Kansas.

George Palmer Putnam Collection of Amelia Earhart Papers, Archives and Special Collections, Purdue University Libraries, West Lafayette, Indiana.

Library of Congress (Manuscript Division; Prints and Photographs Division; Science, Technology and Business Division; General Collections), Washington, DC, www.loc.gov.

Schlesinger Library, Radcliffe Institute for Advanced Study, Harvard University, Cambridge, Massachusetts.

Publications

Backus, Jean L. *Letters from Amelia, 1901–1937.* Boston: Beacon Press, 1982.

Butler, Susan. *East to the Dawn: The Life of Amelia Earhart.* Boston: Addison Wesley, 1997.

Earhart, Amelia. *The Fun of It* (1932). Chicago: Academy Chicago Publishers, 1977.

———. *Last Flight* (1937). Three Rivers, Michigan: Three Rivers Press, 1996.

———. *20 Hours, 40 Minutes: Our Flight in the* Friendship (1928). Washington, DC: National Geographic, 2003.

Long, Marie, and Elgen Long. *Amelia Earhart: The Mystery Solved.* New York: Touchstone, 1999.

Lovell, Mary S. *The Sound of Wings.* New York: St. Martin's Press, 1989.

Morrissey, Muriel Earhart, and Carol L. Osborne. *Amelia, My Courageous Sister.* Santa Clara, California: Osborne Publisher, 1987.

Putnam, George Palmer. *Soaring Wings.* Orlando, Florida: Harcourt, Brace and Co., 1939.

Rich, Doris L. *Amelia Earhart: A Biography.* Washington, DC: Smithsonian Institution, 1989.

ACKNOWLEDGMENTS

The author thanks the following people and institutions for their help with this book:

Albert and Gabrielle Bresnik; William Sittig, chief, and Charles Trew, Science, Technology and Business Division, and Tammy Wong, Geography and Map Division, Library of Congress; Kate Igoe, National Air and Space Museum, Smithsonian Institution; Sammie L. Morris and Marietta Taylor at Purdue University Libraries Archives and Special Collections; Jacalyn Blume at the Schlesinger Library, Radcliffe Institute for Advanced Study, Harvard University; Diane Windham Shaw and Elaine Stomber, Skillman Library, Lafayette College; and Helen Jane Williams.

IMAGES

Reproduction numbers, when available, are given for all items in the collections of the Library of Congress. Unless otherwise noted, Library of Congress images are from the Prints and Photographs Division. To order reproductions, note the LC- number provided with the image; where no number exists, note the Library division and the title of the item. Direct your request to:

> The Library of Congress
> Photoduplication Service
> Washington DC 20540-4570
> (202) 707-5640; www.loc.gov